HOW TO STUDY THE BIBLE
[WITH THE GOD WHO WROTE IT]

HOW TO STUDY THE BIBLE
[WITH THE GOD WHO WROTE IT]

Basic Bible Study Process

CONNIE WILLEMS

Come, let us go up to the mountain of the Lord, to the house of the God of Jacob. He will teach us his ways, so that we may walk in his paths.
— Isaiah 2:3

How to Study the Bible (with the God Who Wrote It)

© 2016 by Connie Willems

All rights reserved. No part of this publication may be reproduced in any form without written permission from the author. (RealLifeDiscovery.com)

ISBN: 978-0-9978324-0-2

Unless otherwise identified, all Scripture quotations in this publication are taken from THE HOLY BIBLE, NEW INTERNATIONAL VERSION® NIV® Copyright © 1973, 1978, 1984 by Biblica, Inc.® All rights reserved worldwide.

Other versions used include: The Holy Bible, English Standard Version® (ESV®), Copyright © 2001 by Crossway, a publishing ministry of Good News Publishers. All rights reserved. ESV Text Edition: 2011

Printed in the United States of America

CONTENTS

	Preface	7
	How to Use This Study	9
Week 1	Dig In	13
	Investigate: Map the Passage	
	Interpret: Shift into Neutral	
	Engage: Talk with God	
Week 2	Study with God	31
	Investigate: Observe What's There	
	Interpret: One Main Point	
	Engage: Respond to the Holy Spirit	
Week 3	Taste and See	43
	Investigate: Go on a God Hunt	
	Interpret: Then, Now, Always	
	Engage: Implications and Benefits	
Week 4	Changed in Relationship	55
	Investigate: Find the Experience	
	Interpret: Life with God	
	Engage: Whole-Life Worship	
	How to Keep Studying	69
	Appendix A: Bible Study Resources	71
	Appendix B: Handling Scripture Well	75
	Appendix C: Discerning God's Voice	79
	Help for the Group Leader	83
	Acknowledgments	93
	About the Author	95

PREFACE

This study grew out of a season when I recognized I had been studying the Bible as if God were not in the room.

I had begun to feel I was doing two different kinds of life with God. One was vibrant and active, where I would ask God questions such as, "What are You up to with me?" or "What's important to You here?" Then I'd tune in and expect that God would want to communicate with me. I lived as if God was truly *Immanuel*, "God with us," active and present in every area of my life.

But I was doing Bible study as if God were a distant being who wrote a book, handed it to us, and then gave us some vague, background help through the Holy Spirit while we applied our intellect and common sense to what He had said.

I began exploring what it looked like to do solid, in-depth Bible study that was also deeply relational with the "God Who Is in the Room."

Much of what you see here grew out of that search. Along the way, as I taught classes on how to study the Bible and wrote inductive Bible studies, I shifted my understanding of what I was doing. I was no longer merely studying the Bible. I was studying God Himself, through the book He wrote.

I hope you'll enjoy learning how to study God's book, *with* Him.

—Connie Willems

BASIC BIBLE STUDY PROCESS

PHASE 1
INVESTIGATE
Observe what God recorded for us in His written Word.

- *Week 1* Map the Passage
- *Week 2* Observe What's There
- *Week 3* Go on a God Hunt
- *Week 4* Find the Experience

PHASE 2
INTERPRET
Ask what God meant and why it is significant to Him.

- *Week 1* Shift into Neutral
- *Week 2* One Main Point
- *Week 3* Then, Now, Always
- *Week 4* Life with God

PHASE 3
ENGAGE
Talk with God about how to live out what He has said.

- *Week 1* Talk with God
- *Week 2* Respond to the Holy Spirit
- *Week 3* Implications and Benefits
- *Week 4* Whole-Life Worship

HOW TO USE THIS STUDY

This book will walk you or your group through a basic Bible study process. You'll bring the Bible passage you want to study, and I'll bring the process.

Each week, I'll give you a set of study skills, and you'll practice using them on the passage you have chosen. The next week, we'll cover a different set of tools. By the time you've finished the four weeks, you'll have a whole toolbox full of skills you can use to dig into the Bible for yourself.

The Process

If you're working through this book on your own, you can sit down and do a whole week's study at a time. Or, you might want to spend 15 or 20 minutes working through a study skill and then pick back up with another one the next day.

If you're using the study with a group, you can do the whole study together in your meeting time, with no homework required (though group members can do more practice on their own at home if they wish). You'll simply read the instructions for each skill and then practice it together. See "Help for the Group Leader" at the end of the book for more information.

Bible Passages to Use

You'll get to decide for yourself what passage you'd like to study. I'd suggest starting with something accessible or familiar.

Here are a few things to keep in mind as you choose a passage.

Stay in one place. It's important to study a passage in its context. Stay in one Bible portion so you don't have to orient to a new context each week.

Keep Bible portions on the short side. It seems natural to choose four chapters and cover one a week. However, that will be too much material. Plan to do one fourth to one half of a chapter at a time — you can always add more verses if you have extra time.

Stick with "straightforward" passages. Though almost any Bible passage contains ideas or allusions that can be confusing, don't make the study process unnecessarily difficult. Choose a more familiar Bible portion, such as something from the Gospels or Epistles.

Don't use certain genres. This book covers a basic process and does not deal with the more specialized interpretation needed for books of law (e.g., Leviticus or Deuteronomy), poetry (e.g. Psalms or Proverbs), or prophecy (e.g., Isaiah or Revelation). Therefore, portions from books such as these aren't good fits to use as sample passages.

If you're lost about what passage to choose:
Choose two consecutive chapters from Luke, Acts, Colossians, or Philippians, and do a fourth to a half of a chapter in a session.

Study Resources You'll Need

We'll focus on study skills that don't require background resources. You will, of course, need a Bible (preferably the old-fashioned paper kind!). Other than that, no specialized books are needed. It can be helpful to buy a study Bible as an all-around resource, though that isn't necessary. Many resources are freely available online or in apps.

But beyond that, Bible study isn't about researching lots of books and commentaries. It's about . . . the Bible. So many riches can be unearthed simply from seeing what is right in front of us in the passage. The resources are backup aids; they are not the material we are studying.

During the different weeks, I'll mention when a certain type of resource would be useful for deeper investigation. But for the most part, we'll keep it simple: Bible, pen, and the worksheets in this study guide. Personally, I also like to photocopy or print out the passage I'm studying so I can freely mark, scrawl, and doodle all over it without having those marks in my Bible permanently.

You *Can* Do This!

Even if you're new to Bible study, feel free to dive in and get started. You are allowed to do this on your own, make some mistakes, and learn as you go.

Over time, you'll learn to use the tools and gain background knowledge. In the meantime, it's OK to feel like you don't know what you're doing. Even after doing plenty of Bible study, I can still feel confused when I start from scratch on a section I've never studied.

You may not be the kind of person who loves studying for its own sake — and may never be that way. That's just fine. You may never gather a whole bunch of resources or spend hours at your desk with a pile of books in front of you. That's fine, too.

But do go past the surface. Do listen to the Holy Spirit. Do keep your nose in the Book and your eyes and ears on God. If you do that, then He'll take you where He wants you to go.

If you're leading a group through this study,
see "Help for the Group Leader" at the end of the book.

WEEK ONE

Dig In

You know what? I said to myself a few months ago, *I haven't been outside this small corner of the city for way too long.* My daily routine had taken me along a route between home, work, the grocery store, my errands, and church. All good places, and the necessary stuff of daily life. But I was ready for something more.

Our experience with Bible intake can be similar. We may have a daily routine of reading the Bible for personal growth and encouragement — good and necessary ways to be in God's Word. But we can also hit a point where we're ready for some fresh places.

Since that realization about my routine roads, I've barrelled along open highways under wide blue skies. I've ground my way up switchbacks to the top of high mountain passes. I've spied dirt roads cutting off into the distance, and wondered, *Where does that go?* before taking an unexpected turn to find out — and been glad I did. That kind of exploration and discovery is what I'd wish for you as you go down some new roads with the Bible.

It doesn't take much. Just a basic map — and a Companion.

The Plan

Each week, we'll be moving through a basic plan so you get a feel for the pattern of a typical Bible study. We'll do one study segment in each of the following phases:

PHASE 1	PHASE 2	PHASE 3
INVESTIGATE	**INTERPRET**	**ENGAGE**
Observe what God recorded for us in His written Word.	*Ask what God meant and why it is significant to Him.*	*Talk with God about how to live out what He has said.*

Phase 1: Investigate. Bible study always starts with investigation, where we spend time observing the passage itself closely and carefully.

Phase 2: Interpret. In the second phase, interpretation, we'll begin to draw conclusions about what God meant with the passage.

These first two phases are what sets Bible study apart from Bible intake in other ways, such as reading a passage during a devotional time or meditating on a passage.

Phase 3: Engage. It's not until the third phase that we begin to ask, "What does God have for me personally through this passage?" Sometimes we talk of this phase in terms of making an application of the Bible to our lives. However, our goal here goes beyond finding a principle or truth to apply. We want to engage with God Himself so that He is the one who guides how His Word transforms us.

These three phases undergird most Bible study methods. But there is something more to consider as we get started: our Companion.

The Relationship

While the process of study is important, our concept of Bible study is even more fundamental. For many of us, the word *study* brings to mind sitting at a desk trying to absorb information from a whole bunch of books. It's the school model we're familiar with, and one that we often carry over to studying the Bible. But I believe something different is happening with Bible study. There, we're sitting with the book's Author, looking together at what He wrote.

That expands our approach. In "school" type studying, we engage our minds and learn information, detect outlines, and identify principles. These are necessary skills, and for years I practiced these key aspects of Bible study.

Then, I realized that the God I loved, who wrote this book, was actually "in the room" with me as I studied, through His indwelling Holy Spirit. Study was no longer limited to what I could learn on my own, with my mind. I also could engage my heart and enjoy relationship with God. Whether I was discovering more about ancient Israel or about the early church, I could do the whole study in close connection with God. The Holy Spirit would be the one to reveal His Word and show me His ways, just as Jesus promised He would (John 14:26, 16:14-15).

When we study this way, we become like the people in Isaiah 2, who say to each other, "Come, let us go up to the mountain of the Lord, to the house of the God of Jacob. He will teach us his ways, so that we may walk in His paths" (verse 3). That's why, throughout this study, we'll stop often to talk with God and ask Him what He wants us to see. We'll tell Him how His Word affects us, and we'll invite Him to speak with us in return.

Dive In

Are you ready to get started? On the following pages, you'll find exercises that walk you through this week's skills. Read the instructions for the skill, and then use the space provided to practice it.

If you usually read the Bible for personal growth or relationship with God, you may need to consciously adjust to a more drawn-out process as we get started. This week, we'll emphasize the first two phases of study where we investigate and ask questions. We will also relate with God, but we won't yet draw any firm conclusions about the passage or look for personal applications from it (that will come in later weeks).

This week, we'll practice the following study skills:

1. ***Investigate***   Map the Passage
2. ***Interpret***   Shift into Neutral
3. ***Engage***   Talk with God

Phase 1: Investigate

Map the Passage

We'll start our study skills in the investigation phase. The first things we want to investigate regarding any passage are its context and content: What kind of book are we reading? What comes before and after the passage? What are the main portions within the passage? This information is key to understanding what the passage means.

How to Do It

You'll focus in two areas here: the passage's context and content. You could spend a great deal of time doing this, so pace yourself according to the depth of study you're doing. If you're practicing with a group, you will only have time for a brief look.

Context

Investigating the context means you consider what surrounds your passage.

- **Book.** Look at the first paragraphs of the book your passage is in, and then turn to the end of the book and look at the last paragraphs. Some books of the Bible will give clues in these locations about the author, the reason for writing, the time period, or the type of writing (such as history, a letter, or a biography). Not every book will do this.
- **Passage.** Look at the text that surrounds your passage. Are you in the middle of a thought or story, or are you at the start of one?
- **Background.** If you have more time, check to see if your Bible has study notes at the beginning of your passage's book, and look for the author, setting, and history. All study Bibles will have this information, as will many other Bibles. But don't go

here first — start by exploring on your own. (For information on study Bibles, see Appendix A, Bible Study Resources.)

Content

Next, you want an overview of your passage's content. Look within your passage, and list the major "pieces" of thought or the scenes in the historical account. You don't need to rely on your Bible's paragraphs here — sometimes there will be a couple of thought portions in one paragraph or one portion may cover several paragraphs.

Practice It

Before You Start: Have you chosen a portion of the Bible to work with? If not, see "Bible Passages to Use" in the "How to Use This Study" information at the beginning of this book.

1. **Context.** Ask God, "Will You help me notice what You want me to see?" Then look at the first paragraphs of the book your passage is in, and flip to the end of the book and look at the last paragraphs. Write what you can find about the book your passage is in.

Author(s)

Type of writing (laws/legal; historical accounts; proverbs; poetry or songs; letters; prophetic dreams, visions, or messages)

Any clues about the book's time frame or purpose

2. Scan through your passage's context. What comes . . .

   before it?

   after it?

3. **Content.** Make a list of the major portions within your passage.

   Example, from Acts:
   17:16-21 — Paul and philosophers start a dialogue.
   17:22-23 — Paul says he knows their unknown god.

Phase 2: Interpret

Shift into Neutral

You'll do more investigation than we just did when you study a passage, but for now, we'll move on to the second study phase. In the interpretation phase, we draw conclusions about what the passage means.

The first skill we want to learn is to approach the passage as neutrally as possible. We want to slow down, recognize what we already think, acknowledge what we don't know, hold off on adding our opinions, and give God space to open up the passage's meaning to us over time.

Recently, I studied John 15:9-17 with a small group. As we discussed the passage, many of us realized that, quite unknowingly, we had already "pre-interpreted" Jesus' statement in verse 10. He said, "If you obey my commandments, you will remain in my love." We read the verse as if Jesus were saying, "If you *don't* do what I told you to do, I won't love you anymore. My love is conditional on your behavior." We weren't neutral! We were bringing some misconceptions about God's love to what Jesus said. If we hadn't slowed down to recognize what we were bringing with us, we could easily have misinterpreted the passage. Shifting into neutral gave us space to step back and do more investigation of what Jesus was *actually* saying.

How to Do It

Staying neutral is simple when we don't understand the passage at all; it's more difficult when the passage's meaning seems plain. It can be even harder when we've gotten a burst of insight and are excited about what we've seen. Here are some helps for making the shift.

Notice what you already know. If you've heard teaching on the passage or have studied it personally, note what you already think about it. (This doesn't mean your thinking is wrong; you're just noting where you currently are — like putting an "I am here" pin into a map.)

Notice personal responses that color how you view the passage. Maybe the passage has always confused you. Maybe God used it powerfully and personally with you and now you always see it in terms of that experience. Maybe you don't find it particularly interesting or relevant. Maybe it presents a view of God or a teaching that you find difficult. All these responses can affect how you interpret.

Notice what you don't know. One of the best ways to shift into neutral is to get curious. It moves your attention from what you already know or think to what you don't know. This slows you down and puts you into the mindset of a learner. Even if the passage is familiar, find questions to ask about it. Maybe there are historical references you don't understand or terms you haven't heard. If the passage is very familiar, put yourself into the mindset of a brand-new believer with no Bible experience: What questions would you have about it then?

Practice It

1. Deliberately connect with God as you begin to interact with His Words. Use the prayer below, or write in one of your own.

> *"God, I want to be like the people described in Isaiah 2 who want You to teach them Your ways so they can walk in Your paths. But especially, I want to know You. Will You help me with that, giving me Your Spirit of wisdom and revelation, so I may know You better?"*
>
> *(See Isaiah 2:3 and Ephesians 1:17)*

Personal note: If you're like me, you might be tempted to skip prayer steps like the one we just did. Please do stop and take time to pray; talking with God during your study is a key way to engage personally with Him and keep from relying on your own thoughts or study abilities.

2. Make notes under the following prompts.

Here is what I already think about this passage . . .

Here is how I respond to it personally . . .

Here are the questions I have or the things I wonder about . . .

Follow-Up: What to Do with Your Questions

- Questions often signal a place to do more investigation. If you want to study one of your questions now, read the passage and its context several more times. Sometimes more familiarity can answer questions. You can also look up cross-references to see if other passages shed light, or check out some background information. (Cross-references are those passages listed in your Bible's center margin or footnotes. See Appendix A for more Bible study resources you can use).

- Talk with God about your questions, but know that He rarely answers questions on a schedule. That's OK! The Bible isn't going anywhere; God's not going anywhere. You can relax into taking time with Him about His Word.

Phase 3: Engage

Talk with God

After practicing the first two phases of Bible study (investigation and interpretation), we're ready for the third phase: engage. Since we are doing Bible study *with* God, we want to be deliberate about turning to Him during each study session to share our thoughts and hearts with Him and open space for Him to share His with us.

A good way to start this conversation is to talk with God about what we've studied. Sometimes we'll tell Him how a passage has affected us: "God, when I see that You are the God of all comfort, I feel hopeful" (see 2 Corinthians 1:3). At other times, we'll simply tell Him our thoughts and feelings, just as we'd do if a close Friend were sitting and studying with us.

How to Do It

When we get deeper into a study, we'll talk with God about how He would like to change us through His Word. At the beginning of studying a passage (as we are now), we'll often simply relate with Him (which, of course, always changes us).

Share openly. The key to relationship is to open up and share with God about where we are "below the surface." An above-the-surface prayer might sound like this:

> *God, I want to know Scripture better and grow as I study Ephesians.*

A prayer that goes below the surface is more open about emotions and thoughts. It might sound like this:

> *God, I'm a little intimidated as I start Ephesians. I'm not really the studying type, and I often feel stupid around people who*

know more about the Bible than I do. But I know that feeling isn't from You. I want to get started because I think I'm going to get to know You better — and I think I really would like to know more about the Bible.

Allow space for God to talk. Make sure to give God an opening to bring His thoughts or impressions to your mind or heart in response to what you've said to Him. (Often, we say something to God and then go off and do the next thing, without waiting to see if He would like to talk with us.)

Practice It

1. Choose one of the following prompts (or use one of your own) and use it as an opening to write down what you want to say to God.

- ❏ "God, I chose this passage because _____. Here is what I am hoping for as I study it . . . "
- ❏ "God, I'm feeling _____* about learning how to study Your words to me."
- ❏ "Father, I wish I felt more ready to do this studying, but here is what is going on with me . . . "
- ❏ "God, I felt _____* as I studied this passage . . . "

2. Pause and give God space to respond to what You've said to Him; He often does this by bringing a thought or impression into our minds or hearts. Write down what you sense He might be wanting you to know. (See Appendix C for information on discerning God's voice.) There's no pressure here to "have to" hear from God or make anything happen — just pause and give Him your attention. If you don't sense anything, that's fine. Feel free to leave the space blank.

*Emotion words to help you fill in the blanks
Sharing our emotions with God is a sure way to go below the surface with Him. Feel free to be open with what you're actually feeling (even if it seems different from what you "should" feel). Here are some emotions you might feel as you study:

fearful	stupid	eager	helped
disappointed	bored	challenged	cared for
angry	confused	awed	peaceful
rejected	doubtful	grateful	joyful
guilty	overwhelmed	encouraged	energized
convicted	longing	hopeful	secure
condemned	interested	loved	accepted

Week 1: Wrap-Up

That wraps up our Bible-study practice for this week. We've gained the following skills:

PHASE 1 INVESTIGATE	PHASE 2 INTERPRET	PHASE 3 ENGAGE
• Map the Passage	• Shift into Neutral	• Talk with God

If you are used to reading the Bible for personal application or doing Bible study lessons that close with application, you might be feeling a little unsatisfied right now. After all, we barely scratched the surface of the passage, we opened up more questions than we answered, and we didn't get into application at all. Never fear. This week was about learning some introductory skills and beginning to talk with God about His Book. Next week we'll pick back up with the passage and go more deeply into it.

Bible study will have a big pay-off, both in answering questions and transforming our lives, but it often happens more slowly than other kinds of Bible intake. In the meantime, remember that you never have to wait to relate with the God who wrote it.

A Personal Word

Over the decades since I first began learning about the Bible, I've experienced two key shifts regarding it. The first was fairly simple: I went from feeling confused much of the time to a place where the

Bible themes, people, and timelines began to sort themselves out and make sense. This shift came gradually as I gained information and experience.

The second shift came when I moved from studying the Bible on my own to studying God's words *with* Him. In that season, I started to look for ways to be as relational with God during Bible study as I was when I was talking with Him during my normal day.

One day, as I was making Bible study notes along the lines of, "God does . . ." and "God thinks . . ." and "God did . . ." I realized I was talking about God in the third person, as if He were a distant, far-away being. Not as if He were right there with me. So I began writing my notes differently. I'd jot down notes as if I were talking to Him personally: "You do . . ." and "You think . . ." That shift alone made the study more personal. I was discovering Bible study with God at my side.

I became even more personal than that and began to "chat" with God throughout my study. In fact, if you were to see my Bible study notes these days, you'd see observations about the passage interspersed with comments I wrote directly to God.

Sometimes I'll stop and ask questions about what I don't understand. "What was going on there?" I'll ask God. "I'm confused."

When I need to, I'll be honest, and say, "God, I have to admit I'm put off by the actions I see in this passage. They don't make sense to my 21st-century mindset, and I'm struggling with the idea that this is something You do. I need help here!"

I don't plow through these difficult passages alone. I expect that the Holy Spirit will welcome my questions and guide me as I wrestle through them. These questions aren't always resolved quickly, and I feel a tension as I'm both close to God and asking questions about His written words. But that's a good tension: I'm taking what He has said and who He is seriously.

Sometimes my comments to God are personal. "God, look how these people turned against You. That must have grieved You so much." Or I tell Him, "God, look at what You did here! That was wonderful!"

At these times, I can almost sense Him grinning and saying, "That's nothing, kid . . . wait until you see what I have for you in the next paragraph!"

I'm certainly enjoying Bible study more with this relational approach — and I suspect that God is enjoying the time with me more as well.

WEEK TWO

Study with God

One of the biggest barriers many of us face with Bible study is not in learning the skills for it, but in learning to approach it relationally. It's easy to deal only with facts and principles.

I did this just today; I wanted to do some study but didn't have a lot of time. So I gave the passage a scan, looked for a few facts, and was ready to move on.

Then I heard God's quiet whisper, "Are you going to talk with Me about any of that?"

I sighed. Actually, I hadn't even thought about opening up space to talk with God. I was in task mode. I wanted to get on with my day. But to treat the Bible as just a book and to treat God as if He weren't right there with me? I couldn't do that, either. So I slowed down and talked with Him.

Sometimes, a quick scan is all I have space for. But if that becomes my norm, it's like only eating nutritional supplements and calling them a meal. Whole-life Bible intake at God's side is a feast, with the best dinner-table conversation we've ever had.

Dive In

Like last week, this week will take you through all three phases of Bible study.

You'll start with investigation, where you simply observe what is in the passage. Then, in interpretation, you will draw conclusions about meaning. Finally, you will engage with God personally. Use the same verses you studied last week so you can get a more complete understanding of that passage.

This week, you'll practice the following study skills:

1. ***Investigate***   Observe What's There
2. ***Interpret***   One Main Point
3. ***Engage***   Respond to the Holy Spirit

Phase 1: Investigate

Observe What's There

Last week, we mapped the context and content of the passage. This week, we'll use the same passage and look for smaller elements. To put it simply, we're going to "see what we can see."

If you're studying the book of Luke, maybe you'll notice and list the types of questions Jesus asks. If you're in an epistle, maybe you'll underline all the times the phrase "in Christ" is used. If you're in Ruth, you might circle the different names for God within your passage and note which person uses which name.

The more time you spend sifting a passage and noticing what's there, the more you'll find. In fact, this kind of careful, in-depth observation is central to good Bible study.

How to Do It

Scan the passage and look for the following types of elements:

- Repeated words or phrases
- Key people and events
- Central ideas or terms
- Emotions or descriptions
- Context markers that link portions together, such as *therefore, in the same way, then,* or *the next day*
- Actions or verbs
- Contrasts (introduced by words such as *but* or *however*; or contrasts such as light versus darkness)
- Symbols or word pictures
- Lists

- Causes and effects
- Patterns or processes
- Anything that seems unusual or striking to you

If you can, also read the passage aloud — sometimes hearing it will help you notice elements you might skim past in silent reading.

Practice It

1. Scan through or read aloud the passage you used last week, looking for the types of nuggets on the previous list. You could spend a lot of time here, so pace yourself. Start with one or two items. Then, if you have more time, scan again looking for another item. Write down whatever you notice.

2. Now that you've made a list, ask God to add to it. Choose one of the following prompts, and write in the rest of your prayer.

- ❑ "Father, I know what I saw, but I may have overlooked what's important to You here . . ."
- ❑ "God, this is Your book, so You are the one who knows what's in it . . ."

3. Then do another scan, expecting that God will bring His thoughts to your mind. Add more items to your list.

Phase 2: Interpret

One Main Point

Now that we've practiced some investigation, we want to move to the second phase of Bible study: interpretation. Bible study separates these two phases because it's important to grasp the passage's content before we draw conclusions about it. This slows us down and helps us keep our personal interpretations out of the mix. Since these are God's words, we want to know what *He* intended the passage to say or mean.

One way to practice interpretation is to sum up the main point of the passage in one or two sentences. This skill helps us remember what the passage is about and checks how much of the passage's meaning we grasp — it's hard to find words for something we don't understand!

How to Do It

In this practice, you will first ask the Holy Spirit for His thoughts and wisdom, and then restate the main point of the passage in one or two sentences. As you do this, remember to:

- Assume the plain, normal meaning of the passage in its context before looking for symbolic or figurative meanings.
- Stick to what the passage in front of you *actually* says.
- For now, keep yourself from adding in meanings or information that you know from listening to teachers or from studying other passages that relate to yours.

Practice It

1. Before you begin, consider how you need the Holy Spirit to help you as you do this exercise. List the ways (your list may be long or short).

2. Write one or two sentences about the passage's main point. Be as informal or casual in your language as you like — talk the way you normally do.

The main point of this passage is . . .

Follow-Up: Clearing Up Confusion

If you drew a blank when you tried summarizing, that doesn't mean you're doing something wrong or can't do Bible study. It may merely signal a need for more investigation.

You could read the passage a couple more times, read the notes in your study Bible, look up confusing terms in a Bible dictionary, or consult a commentary. (See Appendix A for information on where to find some of these resources.)

Phase 3: Engage

Respond to the Holy Spirit

In the third phase of Bible study, we engage with God. These are God's words, so we want to talk them over with Him and let Him apply them to our lives. God's Holy Spirit — our Counselor, Advocate, Helper, Comforter, and Encourager — lives with us and knows exactly what we need. He may point out:

> A way of thinking He wants us to adopt
> Something new He wants us to experience with Father God
> Something He wants us to start praying about or asking for
> A reason to praise or celebrate with God
> A habit He'd like us to begin practicing — or give up
> An adventure He wants to take us on
> Something He wants to give us, such as encouragement, hope, resources, or abilities
> An area where He wants to free us from sin
> A way He wants us to join in the work He is doing around us
> A way He is pleased and delighted with us

The key is that we move our focus from figuring out right actions on our own to discerning God's voice and responding to Him. When He has our attention and our "Yes," He can do in us all He has in mind for us.

How to Do It

We could spend entire books talking about how to follow God in this responsive way! But these simple steps will get us started.

Ask. Turn to God, ask Him to reveal to you what He would like you to see or know, and expect that He wants to do this with you.

Practice discerning. The Holy Spirit lives with us and testifies to our spirits that we are God's children (see Romans 8:16). We are to walk with the Spirit, keep in step with Him, and follow Him. This means we need to practice detecting what He is saying and doing. Begin to notice the ways God speaks to you, nudges you, and guides you.

Respond. Our response is key. When you sense God speaking to you, reply to Him. When you sense Him prompting you in one of the areas above, say "yes" and move toward that thought or action. Of course, it's not always this easy; sometimes the more honest starting place is, "God, help me be willing to be willing!"

Practice It

1. **Ask.** Below, write your prayer sharing your response to the passage with God and asking Him to highlight for you what He especially wants you to see or know from what you've studied.

"Father, here is how I was feeling as I started this study:

As I studied, I felt especially drawn to:

Will You bring Your thoughts about this passage to my mind and heart?"

2. **Practice discerning.** Review your notes, trusting that the Holy Spirit does want to speak with you. He might bring a thought or sentence to your mind. He might "highlight" something in your notes. You might have a "sense" or "impression," such as, *Here . . . this is the part that is*

important. You might remember something that stood out to you as you studied.

Note: You won't necessarily feel something "special" or have a great spiritual experience here. The Holy Spirit's communication is often quite ordinary. (See Appendix C for information on hearing God.) Below, write down whatever you sense from Him.

3. **Respond.** Write your response to God. If you didn't seem to sense anything from Him, simply tell Him that, and go on to tell Him more of your thoughts or feelings about what you studied.

Week 2: Wrap-Up

We've now had a couple of weeks of practice moving through a basic Bible study process. Over the past two weeks, we have used the following skills:

PHASE 1 INVESTIGATE	PHASE 2 INTERPRET	PHASE 3 ENGAGE
• Map the Passage • Observe What's There	• Shift into Neutral • One Main Point	• Talk with God • Respond to the Holy Spirit

If you're studying with a group, you can go home and practice these skills on a different passage. As you practice them, they will start to become second nature, and you'll find yourself digging just a bit deeper into the Bible without working to do it.

A Personal Word

The majority of Bible study instructions I've read open with something to the effect of, "Pray and ask the Holy Spirit to guide you as you do your study." *That's good*, I would think, as I nodded along at how right that sounded.

But did I ever stop and pray a prayer like that before I started to study — or any kind of prayer, for that matter? True confession: I never did. I just kept reading so I could get to the "real" part of the study.

There were a couple of reasons I fell into this. First, I just didn't have any practical knowledge of the difference between leaning on my own understanding and leaning on God's. If you'd pressed me about what to expect the Holy Spirit's guidance to be like, I'd have been forced to say, "I'm not sure; I guess I'm just supposed to pray and then go on like normal, assuming God is doing something."

The second reason would have been more subtle. I had a strong trust in "solid thinking" and "sound skills" and an (unspoken) distrust of the Holy Spirit. Somewhere way in the background of my mind was a notion that surely it would be risky to leave someone alone with only the Bible and the Holy Spirit — who knows what kind of error would result! (God, forgive me for thinking that of Your Spirit!)

I remember the day when I made the connection that should have been obvious: The Holy Spirit *authored* the Bible (2 Peter 1:20-21). Therefore, He is absolutely trustworthy with it. There's no distinction between a life solidly grounded on Scripture and a life intimately led by the Spirit. We can lean on Him to interpret His Word to us and lead us into "all truth," just as Jesus promised He would (John 16:13).

The reality is, the more I practice detecting the Holy Spirit's voice and studying with Him,

- the more solid my thinking becomes, because it is being transformed to match His. He shifts my reliance from my own smarts onto His wisdom.
- the hungrier I am for the Bible, because that's where I can always find and experience the life of God.
- the more alive, enjoyable, and adventurous my Christian life becomes.

And yes, now I actually stop to pray when I study. In God's company, I am experiencing the reality of the Book, not just reading or studying it.

WEEK THREE

Taste and See

A few months ago, God sent me into the books of 1 and 2 Samuel to look at Kings David and Saul. I dutifully read the books. I was interested, but (I'll admit it) not particularly engaged. So I went back to read them again, figuring I must have missed something. As I did, I asked God, "Why am I doing this? What do You want me to see?"

"Look at how these two men related with Me," He hinted.

Aha! With that lens, I began to see a key difference in these first two kings of Israel. Though Saul ultimately failed to obey God, he also did a great deal of "God stuff": He offered sacrifices, consulted priests to ask God what to do, and talked of obeying God's commands.

But David . . . David pursued God Himself. He talked about God and to God as if he knew Him personally: "You are beautiful. Loving. Compassionate." He found the law life-giving because he found God there. (See Psalms 27:4; 86:5,15; and 19:7.)

No wonder David found God's words as sweet as honey when he took them in (19:10). He wasn't merely obeying commands. He was taking in God Himself. "Taste and see," David urged, "that the LORD is good" (34:8).

That's what we want to bring to our study of God's words: an eager desire for God Himself.

Dive In

As we did last week, we'll move through all three phases of Bible study this week. First, we'll investigate the experience embedded in a passage, then we'll practice interpreting, and finally we'll engage with God about the passage's implications and benefits.

You can continue with the same set of verses you've been studying the last two weeks, or, if you have a fairly good understanding of them by now, you can move on to the next portion of your passage.

This week, we'll practice the following study skills:

1. Investigate   Go on a God Hunt
2. Interpret   Then, Now, Always
3. Engage   Implications and Benefits

Phase 1: Investigate

Go on a God Hunt

This week we're going to practice investigation by sifting through the passage for what we can discover about God. We want to be deliberate about looking for who He is, what He cares about, and what He does. This is my favorite study practice we'll cover, because it is the one where we most directly discover and get to know God.

How to Do It

Read through your passage. Look for, and circle or list:

- Mentions of God, Father, Son, Jesus, Christ, or the Holy Spirit (and, in the Old Testament, Angel of the LORD, which can refer to God).
- Names or attributes of God (e.g., Most High, King of kings, Son of man, shepherd, glorious, compassionate)
- Words or phrases that allude to who God is or what He does without plainly saying it. For example, Paul says in Galatians 5:13, "You . . . were called to be free," but he does not say who did the calling. When the Holy Spirit helps us notice a mention such as this, we fill in the blank and realize, "God calls us to freedom."

Practice It

1. Since we're studying God, we want to let Him reveal Himself to us. Below, I've personalized the prayer in Ephesians 1 for you. Read the personalization, and then use the prompt to write your response back to God.

God's heart for you: *"I, the God of your Lord Jesus Christ, your glorious Father, want to give you My Spirit of wisdom and revelation so you can know Me better. I want to enlighten the eyes of your heart in order that you may know the hope to which I have called you, the riches of My glorious inheritance in My saints, and My incomparably great power for you." (See Ephesians 1:17-19.)*

Your response: *"Glorious Father, I'm getting ready to look for You in Your Word. When I hear what You want to do for me, I [feel / want / think] . . .*

2. ***Your investigation.*** If you are starting with a new passage this week, make sure you know the passage's context and that you read it over a couple of times to familiarize yourself with it. (You might want to review "Map the Passage" from week one.)

Then look for the mentions of God. List the reference and note the fact about God; or note what God says, does, thinks, or feels.

Example, from Titus:
 2:11 — God made His grace appear to all people.
 2:13 — Jesus Christ will appear.
 3:4-5 — God saved us when His kindness and love appeared.

(notes, cont'd)

Phase 2: Interpret

Then, Now, Always

Now that we've done a layer of investigation, it's time to move into the interpretation phase of study. This time, we'll consider the passage in light of *then*, *now*, and *always*.

Some passages contain elements specific to a time, person, or culture (*then*). In these cases, we consider how our situations are similar or different (*now*). Finally, we look for the underlying truth that applies for all time (*always*).

How to Do It

Look at the passage with the following lenses:

> ***Then:*** Is there anything in the passage specific to the time or culture in which it was written?
> ***Now:*** How is our situation today similar or different?
> ***Always:*** What does not change, no matter the time or culture? (These are generally truths about God's nature or ways.)

Practice It

1. Before you begin, talk with God: "Father, I want to see this passage the way You intended it to be seen. I want Your thoughts and viewpoints regarding it."

2. Then write your answers to the following questions.

> ***Then and Now:*** How is our situation today similar to that of the passage? How is it different?

Always: *What truths from the passage apply no matter what the time or culture?*

Follow-Up: Difficult Interpretations
Sometimes this exercise highlights thorny interpretation questions. See "Handling Scripture Well" (Appendix B) for information on interpretation.

Phase 3: Engage

Implications and Benefits

We're ready to practice the final phase of Bible study: engaging honestly with God about the passage. Here, we'll consider the implications of what we've seen. Bible study can be — and should be — transforming. When God speaks, His words open doorways to change. The question is, will we walk through?

It may seem that the answer is, "Of course!" And that is the ultimate outcome we're aiming for. But part of making that decision real is to look at the implications of God's words and ways. This allows God to surface not only the "right" choice we know we should make, but the real-life realities it brings.

How to Do It

Answer one or more of the following types of questions about your passage. You'll look at the implications from your perspective and then consider them from God's viewpoint.

- *Your perspective:* What are the risks of living like the passage portrays? What risk do we take if we do not live this way? What are the costs of taking this seriously? What benefit does it bring?
- *God's perspective:* What might God say is at risk in your life regarding this passage? How might God view the costs associated with this passage? What resources might He have for you?

Notice that these questions aren't yet calling for a commitment to change. They are designed to give the Holy Spirit space to speak with us about the realities of life in God's world.

Practice It

1. Choose one or two of the questions to answer. (Not every question will apply to every passage.)

Also, if you are dealing with a complex passage, such as the Sermon on the Mount, you may need to choose one sentence or verse to focus on. Don't overwhelm yourself by trying to deal with the implications of the entire passage.

The answer to the question from my perspective:

How this question might be answered from God's perspective:

2. Ask, "God, what would You like to say to me about this?" Then pause and allow Him time to respond. Write down what You sense Him saying.

Week 3: Wrap-Up

We added a few more tools to our Bible study toolkit this week and now have a variety of ways to investigate, interpret, and engage with God and the Bible. Here is what we've covered so far:

PHASE 1 INVESTIGATE	PHASE 2 INTERPRET	PHASE 3 ENGAGE
• Map the Passage	• Shift into Neutral	• Talk with God
• Observe What's There	• One Main Point	• Respond to the Holy Spirit
• Go on a God Hunt	• Then, Now, Always	• Implications and Benefits

You can come back and use these tools again and again on different passages. When you do, you don't have to use them in the order we've done here. Do start with investigating the passage's context, and then choose more tools to complete your study.

A Personal Word

I'm glad that, along with David's eager desire for God and His words, we also have records of times when David felt distant from God and wondered where He was (see, for example, Psalms 13 and 22). It helps me to feel more normal when my hunger for God lags or my desire for the Bible wavers.

These days, I am coming out of a non-hungry time. Sure, I kept reading the Bible. And I studied passages for teaching or researching. But I was only mildly interested. I kept up Bible intake mostly as a preventative from disconnecting altogether (not a bad motive — go away too far and it's harder to come back).

The Holy Spirit has had something more in store for me, it would seem. I've been hungry for the Bible the past couple of weeks. Almost ravenous. It feels somewhat like the kind of hunger David talked about. Not only am I eagerly reading whole books at a time, I've caught myself thinking, *I get to read 2 Thessalonians this evening!*

I know that sounds as if I'm hyper-spiritual, but trust me — I'm not. I just can't generate this type of hunger on my own. Left to myself, the best I can do is, "I *should* be in the Bible," or "I need to," or "I have to." Never, "I get to." This hunger is a stirring of God's Spirit in me. (In fact, I think it must make the Holy Spirit happy to stir His people toward the Word. After all, He's the one who inspired it in the first place!)

Another way my hunger for God stirs is when I experience Him working and acting in the ways I see in Scripture. For many years, John 15:5 was a bland verse for me. There, Jesus says, "I am the vine; you are the branches. If a man remains in me and I in him, he will bear much fruit; apart from me you can do nothing." Not only did I have zero practical experience of "remaining" in Christ, I had heard that verse so often it became what I call a slogan verse — a quote to put on a pretty picture of vines and grapes, but nothing more.

Then, God took me through a season of showing me what deep abiding looked like, of what it could mean to go through a day in ordinary conversation and connection with Him. In that season, I read John 15 and thought, *I get it now — that verse is real! It's not just some pretty saying for a poster. That's how life with God works.*

Now that I've tasted God in this way, it would be hard to go back to a life without Him. Maybe that's why David urges us to "taste and see." When we do, we're "ruined" for any other way of living.

WEEK FOUR

Changed in Relationship

You may have noticed that, so far, the skills we've learned haven't asked you to commit to major life changes as you apply your Bible passages. There's a practical reason for this: Many Christians are in the Bible during the week, whether for devotional reading or for study. In addition, they probably hear a sermon on Sunday at church. Some are also in small-group studies. Each reading, sermon, and study usually brings up something to apply, change, or do.

But here's the reality: We can't make two or three *genuine* life changes a week. I certainly can't. (I can barely manage one a month!) If every study or sermon calls for big changes and applications, I eventually stop taking them to heart and just let them bounce off me. I can't keep up.

That's why, in this study, I am emphasizing the sure-fire route I've found to Bible application: Take in God's words, talk with Him about them, and then follow His lead. Of all the areas where I *could* be changing, He knows the one or two where He wants to focus. Sometimes He takes me to a heart area that cuts more deeply than I'd go on my own. At other times, He wants me to experience His companionship or care. Sometimes, He wants to free me up to enjoy and celebrate more.

You can trust Him in the same way. Use your Bible study to learn God's ways and truths. Get familiar with His voice. Talk to Him about the study. Ask Him to share His thoughts and heart with you. Heed what He says, and He will be the one to change your life.

Dive In

Again, we have three new skills to learn this week, using the same three-phase pattern of investigate, interpret, and engage. You can use these skills on the same passage you studied last week or move on to the next section of verses.

This week, we'll practice the following study skills:

1. Investigate   Find the Experience
2. Interpret   Life with God
3. Engage   Whole-Life Worship

Phase 1: Investigate

Find the Experience

In the past weeks' investigation skills, we've looked for:

- the big-picture context of the passage
- nuggets of information within the passage
- who God is and what He does

Though we've separated these ways of investigating in order to learn how to do them, you'll usually blend them together and do all of them on the passage in front of you.

Our next investigation practice will take us to a place that is not as common with Bible study: We'll look for what people were experiencing and feeling.

We limit Bible study if we only look for doctrinal truths or historical facts. This is God's revelation of Himself, and God is relational and expressive. He grieves and rejoices; He feels anger and passion; He is tender and caring. Encountering Him affects people deeply.

When we miss a passage's feeling and emotion, we miss seeing an accurate perspective of what our lives with God might be like. For example, when we study, "Love the Lord your God" (Luke 10:27), looking for the experience means we ask, "Does the word *love* mean God wants us to *feel* affection toward Him?" If we're not looking for the experience or feeling, we may reduce love simply to the actions of "obey" or "follow."

How to Do It

Look for words or phrases that indicate feelings or experiences. Here are some examples of what you might find:

- What people might see, hear, feel, smell, or taste (e.g., "a crowd gathered" means there was noise and commotion — maybe it's hard to hear or see)
- Words that indicate emotions (e.g., *love, hope, joy, comfort, angry, jealous*)
- Adjectives or descriptions (e.g., *dry, strong, late in the day, while it was dark*)
- Intense actions or circumstances (e.g., someone weeping or laughing; a wedding, illness, or funeral; a parent worried about a child; traveling to a new town or new country; famine or drought; attacking armies)

Practice It

1. As you begin, notice what you're feeling. Are you feeling distracted? Tired? Energized? Jot down three words that describe you right now:

-
-
-

2. Now, tell God about what you feel:

"God, I feel _____ right now. The person who wrote this passage and those who first read it were also experiencing real human emotions and senses. And, You reveal what You were feeling and experiencing. I don't merely want to understand the ideas You preserved; I want the whole-life experience You offer. Will You help me notice the emotions, heart, and gut realities here?"

3. Read your passage. Write down any emotions, adjectives, descriptions, or experiences you notice. (If you are starting with a new passage

this week, make sure you know the passage's context and that you read it over a couple of times before you begin.)

Phase 2: Interpret

Life with God

This week we'll practice interpretation by explaining the passage. Specifically, we're going to tell someone else what life in God's world is like. When we study His Words, we learn what He values, what He wants from us, and how He designed the world to work. Telling this to someone else helps us put words to it for ourselves.

How to Do It

Revisit the observations you have made about your passage. Where in them do you see underlying truths about what life is like with God? You might note:

- Attitudes, responses, or actions that God values in His people
- What God expects from leaders, governments, nations, churches, or other groups
- How God wants us to handle practical matters
- Core principles God established (such as, "Give, and it will be given to you," or "Seek and you will find" (Luke 6:38, 11:9)
- What life is like in God's kingdom or under His rule — or what it will be like in the future

Sum up the passage in one or two sentences. Then note the conclusion you can draw from it about the life God desires for us. Here are a couple of examples:

Galatians 1:6-9
Summary: Paul is astonished that people are abandoning the gospel.

Conclusion about life with God: There is one gospel message; we are expected to stay true to it.

Acts 6:1-6
Summary: The early church designated people to care for widows. Conclusion about life with God: He values widows and desires them to be cared for. Doing so is an honored role.

Practice It

1. Use the grid below to sum up your passage and the conclusion you can draw from it about life with God.

   Summary of what the passage says

   Conclusion about life with God

2. Now talk with God about your interpretation of His life. "God, I did my best at putting words to the kind of life You designed for us to live. Is there anything You would like to add or adjust?" Trust that God will

bring His thoughts to your mind through His Spirit. Look back over the conclusion you noted. Is there anything to add?

3. If you are working with a group, share your explanations with each other, or pair up and take turns telling each other about how life works with God.

Phase 3: Engage

Whole-Life Worship

One of the outcomes of a Bible study should be whole-life worship with our hearts and actions. We discover who God is and exclaim in wonder. We see His patterns of thinking and acting and change to be like Him. We surrender our plans and join what He is doing. We are moved by what we see and love Him more. All these responses are grounded in relationship.

There is an unbreakable link between deep love and radical obedience. In our final Engage exercise, we want to engage with God in both sides of that link: Love God. Heed Him. This is worship with our whole selves.

How to Do It

Review your observations and interpretation of the passage. Then engage with God on one or both sides of the love / obedience link.

Love. Consider what you've discovered about God in your passage and express your emotions and heart to Him about it.

- "God, I praise You because You are _____."
- "Father, I am so grateful that You _____."
- "Jesus, when I learn that You _____, I feel . . . "

Heed. Look at the passage you are studying and ask God one or two questions about how to heed what He says:

- "God, how could I live this way this coming week? What help or resources would You like to make available to me?"
- "God, I've been sensing I need to apply this passage in this way: _____. How would You like to add to or clarify that?"

Practice It

1. ***Review.*** Look over your notes from the passage, asking God to help you recall what He has already been whispering to you.

What I have been sensing as I have studied this passage:

2. ***Love.*** Express what you've been sensing to God, focusing on celebrating Him and loving Him for who He is. You might write notes below, or sing, or worship in whatever way is natural for you.

3. ***Heed.*** Now ask, "God, is there anything from this study that you wish me to heed?" Write what you sense from Him.

Week 4: Wrap-Up

We've added the final tools and now have an entire set of basic Bible study skills:

PHASE 1 INVESTIGATE	PHASE 2 INTERPRET	PHASE 3 ENGAGE
• Map the Passage	• Shift into Neutral	• Talk with God
• Observe What's There	• One Main Point	• Respond to the Holy Spirit
• Go on a God Hunt	• Then, Now, Always	• Implications and Benefits
• Find the Experience	• Life with God	• Whole-Life Worship

We could add many more skills that would allow us to do word studies or topical studies, or study a particular person in the Bible. Even so, this basic skill set gives you a good foundation. I hope that studying God in the past four weeks has made you hungry and thirsty for even more!

A Personal Word

Engaging with the experiences embedded in Scripture often brings the realities of life with God front and center to me in new ways.

Just last night, I asked God to do a specific, good thing for me in this coming week. The request bordered on "too big" in my eyes. It's something I can get by without, so I almost hesitated to ask. But I know God is a good Father who does more than we can ask or imagine (Ephesians 3:20). And I know that Jesus often did things for people who sought Him out and asked Him.

Then a thought struck me, as I remembered the people who boldly asked Jesus for help: If I were back in Jesus' day, would I push through a crowd to ask Him to do this thing for me? Would I yell out after Him as He passed by? Would I insist that He help me? I recalled the accounts in Matthew of people who had done just that (see chapters 9, 15, and 20) and imagined myself in those crowds. I realized that no, I wouldn't have had the same determination and courage.

Seeing the real human experience of asking for something revealed how I was viewing God and this request. Though I hadn't put words to it, I apparently thought that it's OK to ask politely and mildly, but it's not OK to make a big, noticeable deal about it. Yet it was often the men and women who planted themselves right in front of Jesus who got the miracle.

I realized it would be an act of trust for me to go straight to Jesus, "look Him in the eye," and ask for what I wanted. Trust that He would welcome me when I came, trust that He would see my need, trust that He would intervene on my behalf.

So I asked God, "What would be an equivalent today of coming to You with confidence, right up to the throne of grace, and asking for Your help in my time of need?" (See Hebrews 4:16.) God answered with a creative way to stand up and ask out loud for what I needed.

I did it. And I felt some of the same nerves the people approaching Jesus might have felt. But I also asked more boldly than I had asked the night before.

Putting myself into the experience of those who encountered Jesus face-to-face had shifted how I encountered Him, too.

Jesus said that the person who loves Him will keep His word and will experience Him and the Father in a close, intimate way: "My

Father will love him, and we will come to him and make our home with him." No matter what God does in response to my request, I have just experienced more of that closeness with Him.

BASIC BIBLE STUDY PROCESS

PHASE 1
INVESTIGATE

Observe what God recorded for us in His written Word.

Week 1   Map the Passage
Week 2   Observe What's There
Week 3   Go on a God Hunt
Week 4   Find the Experience

PHASE 2
INTERPRET

Ask what God meant and why it is significant to Him.

Week 1   Shift into Neutral
Week 2   One Main Point
Week 3   Then, Now, Always
Week 4   Life with God

PHASE 3
ENGAGE

Talk with God about how to live out what He has said.

Week 1   Talk with God
Week 2   Respond to the Holy Spirit
Week 3   Implications and Benefits
Week 4   Whole-Life Worship

A FINAL WORD

How to Keep Studying

You now have a whole set of Bible study tools to help you investigate scripture, interpret it, and engage with God about it. We could add many more tools to the ones we've covered. But what you've learned here is enough to give you a good start.

In this study, we've separated the study methods into small segments in order to learn them. But as you become more familiar with the skills, you'll find yourself blending them together and becoming less structured about how you use them. You don't have to use the tools in the order we did here; feel free to mix and match. Just make sure that you choose skills from each of the three phases.

Following are some ways you might continue to study.

- *Try it again.* You can go back to the beginning of this book and work through it again with a different set of passages. This time you'll be able to shift your focus off learning the tools and simply use the framework to help you focus on the passage.
- *Do simple studies.* Choose one tool from each phase and use them to do a short, one-time study on a passage.
- *Lead someone else.* Choose one of the tools and use it on its own for a simple time in the Bible with a small group or discipleship group. You can even use it with your children.
- *Enhance your devotional reading.* Pick up a tool here or there to add to your personal time with God.
- *Do a full-blown Bible study.* And, of course, you can use some or all of the tools to do a more intensive Bible study on

your own. You may even use all the investigation tools in a row as you go deep into a passage. As you do more intensive study, you'll also want to use more of the Bible study resources described in Appendix A.

When you continue to study, make sure you look for God's life in all of His words. I sometimes imagine that when I open my Bible, I can hear its pages rustling with sounds of His life with us through the ages.

From the front of the Book comes the chorus of creation and the clash of battles. From the middle, the lonely harp of an outcast king singing to His Shepherd and His Shepherd's voice responding.

The clamor of crowds rises from the Gospels, and the Epistles are filled with the scratch of a pen and the clank of chains as Paul writes his letters from prison.

In between, angels sing and God speaks. Restored lepers shout for joy, and kingdoms come crashing down and are built up again.

This book is alive with the words and thoughts and life of God. He brings the words to life in us as well. The Holy Spirit uses them to transform our mindsets, shift our hearts, and communicate God's heart and relationship to us. He uses them to say, "See, this is your God. Love His words because you love Him."

APPENDIX A

Bible Study Resources

Throughout this study, we've emphasized how to study the passage itself without needing outside resources. However, there are many incredibly helpful Bible study resources available. They fall into several broad categories.

Study Bibles. This type of Bible will give you a one-stop source for reference tools: brief commentary, background notes, a concordance, maps, book summaries, and other helps. If you're going to buy anything, I'd suggest you buy one of these.

The ESV or NIV study Bibles are good for study. The NIV Life Application Bible or NLT Study Bible give a more introductory or devotional approach.

You generally have to purchase study Bibles to get digital access, because these Bibles are under copyright. But you can find a few of them online without charge.

Dictionaries. Unlike the dictionaries we used in school, which list brief word definitions, a Bible dictionary will have short summary articles on various topics. They're useful for getting an overview of a person, doctrine, place, or topic. You'll be able to find Bible dictionaries online.

Concordance. Use a concordance to find which passages use specific words. You'll need these when you're doing a topical study or word study. Many online concordances use the numbering system from the Strong's Concordance to cross-reference the English words with their Greek and Hebrew originals. There are multiple online sources: Just search for "Strong's numbers" and you'll pull up a variety.

Commentaries. Commentaries are written by one person or by a team of scholars. They comment on the meanings and interpretations of passages. The notes in your study Bible are an abbreviated commentary.

Note: Most online commentaries are there because they're in the public domain; some may be a hundred or more years old. Beware of getting bogged down in them unless you enjoy more classical reading or scholarship.

Specialized. This is a catch-all category, because so many resources have been published. You can find books of maps, specialized topical references, books packed with background information, Bible survey books, and myriad others. Though I do have a collection of physical books here, I often turn to digital resources when I want specialized information.

Digital Resources

Many of the types of study tools above are readily available (often without charge) in digital versions.

The following sites are the ones I use most frequently for study (some also have apps available):

- *BibleGateway.com.* My default for online Bible reading, audio Bibles, and quick look-ups.
- *BibleStudyTools.com.* Has several of my most-used reference works.
- *BlueLetterBible.com.* My go-to for looking up original languages, because it has some features I like — but you can find many other sources as well.

This list is just a snapshot of what is currently available. Sites and apps come and go, so be sure to search around for more, or ask others for recommendations of what they like to use.

I do want to add some caution about digital resources. First, anyone can put resources online; while many people who do so are credible (and their information is very useful), if you are unfamiliar with a resource or something about it seems "off" to you, it's good to check to see what organization or person is sponsoring it.

Second, the number of Bible study resources available online is overwhelming — you can spend hours browsing links and only begin to scratch the surface. Here is my caution (based on personal experience!): *Do not let tracking down information distract you from getting into the Bible itself.* After a certain point, adding to your pile of background knowledge adds little additional benefit, and it's time to get back to the plain passage.

Also, remember that many online resources are there either because they are in the public domain or through the generosity of a publisher. When you can, look for the more recent resources — they will be easier to grasp than resources written 75 or more years ago. You can often tell a more modern resource because it will have a publisher's name in the title (for example, IVP, Baker, or Zondervan).

Note: I have gathered links to some of my most-used resources on the Resources page at RealLifeDiscovery.com.

APPENDIX B

Handling Scripture Well

As we study God's written words, we want to be the type of person the Apostle Paul commends, who "correctly handles the word of truth" (2 Timothy 2:15). The following principles, which you will find woven throughout this study, are ways we can do that.

Walk through the Bible study phases. We are doing a great deal toward handling a passage well simply by separating the step of investigating the passage from the steps of drawing conclusions and looking for personal applications. Doing these steps in sequence keeps us from leaping straight to interpretations or applications without understanding the passage itself.

Context rules. We always want to study a passage in its textual context (the verses and chapters before and after it) and in its historical context (how the original hearers or readers would have understood it).

Genres differ. We also look at what type of writing it is, such as historical accounts, teaching, proverbs, poetry, or visions. We interpret proverbs, poetry, visions, and parables differently from epistles. We also need to remember that people from a different culture 2,000 or more years ago didn't adhere to the same types of writing structures we expect from Western authors today.

Stick with what the passage actually says. Do your best not to read into a passage what isn't there. As an example, consider all the things we "know" about the account of Christ's birth that simply aren't there. The Bible does not mention an innkeeper, a stable, or three wise men visiting Jesus at the manger. The more familiar a passage is, the more we tend to bring a backlog of teaching and interpretations to it. As you begin your study, do your best to see the passage itself, apart from all that you have heard taught about it.

Look for ordinary meanings first and symbolic meanings in context. Understand the plain meaning to the hearers of the time before looking for figurative meanings or underlying principles. We also study symbols or topics across a variety of passages where they occur before we draw conclusions about them.

Interpret less clear passages with more clear passages. If the same idea is talked about in a passage that is clear and one that is more puzzling or confusing, use the clearer passage to govern meaning.

Interpret one-time mentions in the larger context of the Bible's teaching on the topic. Jesus told one man seeking eternal life to sell all he owned and give it to the poor (Matthew 19). Before concluding that Jesus wants all wealthy people to do that, you would interpret that conversation in light of all God says about money and wealth.

Rely on the Holy Spirit. This is a paradoxical point, because it's only with the Holy Spirit that we can understand God's words. And yet some odd Bible interpretations can come from people who say, "The Holy Spirit gave it to me!" The Holy Spirit is the Spirit of truth (John 16:13), so He is absolutely trustworthy with His Word. We are the ones who must learn how to discern.

Come to interpretation with both confidence ("The Holy Spirit wants to help me understand this") and humility ("I can get things wrong and may need to grow in discernment"). Be careful of fresh interpretations that nobody has ever received before. Run these by a trusted mentor with solid Bible background and experience discerning how God works and speaks.

Keep the essentials in mind. Avoid getting distracted by trying to nail down answers to questions that don't really matter — no matter how interesting they are. For example, going back to Jesus' birth, we picture Jesus being born in a stable, surrounded by animals. I have read an intriguing, and (to me) convincing alternate explanation of the type of building where Joseph and Mary were staying when Jesus was born. I'll admit that every Christmas I'm tempted to trot out the question and my alternate explanation. But I don't, because the truth is . . . there are few situations in which a detail like this would matter. Even if the traditional explanation of the stable and inn is incorrect, to get embroiled in a discussion about it can easily detract from the true point of the account: Jesus was born.

Remember relationship. Obviously, many passages require much more finesse and study than we can deal with in this introductory study. In addition, interpretation issues can be difficult to resolve. We will run into passages that theologians have debated for years. Sadly, Christians have damaged relationships because of differences. Avoid becoming dogmatic about issues that are not central to the faith. Be generous and grace-filled with your brothers and sisters in Christ.

And finally . . . context rules. Yes, it's worth repeating. Many of the off-base Bible interpretations that float around would wilt away if we followed this one guideline and took the historical and textual context into account.

APPENDIX C

Discerning God's Voice

Throughout this study, I have asked you to lean in and listen to what God has to say to you. Let me be very clear: I do not think that what we hear from God replaces the Bible or has the authority of the Bible. The Bible is the standard by which we examine everything we may be hearing.

The process of talking with God is simple: You say something to Him and "listen" for what He wants to say to you. But most of us have a learning curve when it comes to hearing God. Here is some help for getting started.

Give God space to speak. If you're like me, you're probably used to praying in a long (or short) stream of words. You'll need a different pattern in order to hear God: Say one thing and then stop talking. Give God an opening to reply to what you've said. At the start, you'll probably feel awkward, uncomfortable, or blank. That's fine — just give it a try anyway.

Understand what you're listening for. Some people think that "hearing God" means they are expected to hear an audible voice. Though God might speak audibly, generally, the Holy Spirit talks with our hearts/minds in an "internal" voice (for an example, see Romans 8:16). Many people experience this as a thought or picture that comes into their minds. Sometimes the Holy Spirit will bring a Bible passage or a song to mind. These thoughts and pictures may be accompanied by a sense of impact — you might feel stirred or gripped in some way. Many times, though, you won't "feel" anything special at all.

Expect that God wants to speak. I really had to grapple with the idea that God wanted to communicate with me. I didn't stop during prayer to listen for God because a) I'd never seen it done, b) I had no concept God would speak in the moment, and, even if He did, c) I wouldn't dream of putting God on the spot or "demanding" that He speak. Later, I found time after time in the Bible where God conversed with people, which strengthened my understanding that He does talk with us. And the more I came to know Him, the more I found that He is often more ready to speak than I am to listen! (Note: This doesn't mean He answers questions or provides information on our schedules.)

Keep a record. Write down what you sense God may be saying to you. This not only helps you remember, it's helpful later when you're discerning if you heard accurately.

Expect some uncertainty. "How do I know it's really God?" is one of the primary questions people ask. The answer is that you compare what you're hearing to what God has revealed in the Bible. Everything you hear must be under the authority of Scripture. Even so, you'll experience uncertainty. That's OK. Make note of what you think God may be saying, and ask mature believers to help you grow in discernment.

Cultivate discernment instead of skepticism. Discernment is healthy and necessary. But skepticism will block your ability to respond to God's faint "whispers." *The best way to cultivate discernment is to do exactly what we're doing in this study: Saturate yourself with the Bible.* Study it, read it, enjoy it, and discover who God is from it. Also seek out people who are mature in God and will help you mature in Him.

Listen for relationship. We often default to asking God what to do, forgetting that His primary desire is that we love Him (Luke 10:27). As He talks with you, expect Him to relate with you — to share His love, His affection, His encouragement.

Know that a good God is with you in this. You already have the most important "thing" you need: God's involvement. God devotes an immense amount of attention to you. In fact, through His Holy Spirit,

He lives with you 24/7. He is your Shepherd, your Counselor, your Father, your King.

Trust that He wants to guide you and that He wants you to hear Him accurately. Ask Him to block all other influences and help you hear only Him.

Because what God says will line up with who He is as revealed in the Bible, expect His words to you to be life-giving, kind, loving, patient, full of grace and mercy, compassionate, joyful, peaceful, affectionate, redemptive, hopeful, wise, encouraging, creative, and forgiving. Yes, He will also challenge, convict, and correct, but even His correction will be in line with these qualities.

LEADER GUIDE

Help for the Group Leader

You don't need to be a Bible study expert to lead this study — just be willing to dive in and learn along with those in your group. Following are some things to keep in mind as you lead.

Decide Where to Focus

You can use this book in two ways:

> Focus 1: Use it to teach group members how to study the Bible.
> Focus 2: Use it as a framework for a group Bible discussion that doesn't need a lot of advance preparation.

In the first focus, your discussions will emphasize learning how to study. The Bible passage you use will serve as an example as you practice and discuss the tools.

In the second focus, your discussions will center on the passage itself. The tools will merely be aids that give you a simple way to get the group into a Bible passage and generate solid discussion. If group members pick up some study skills along the way, that's a bonus.

You might find this second focus especially helpful for a community group or life group where you want to include solid Bible content but don't have a leader or teacher who is able to spend hours preparing.

Many groups find it helpful to use the study one time through with the first focus. Then the leader can move to the second focus and begin to use the skills as a way to provide structure for a time of Bible content or discussion. For example, one week you might have only 20 minutes for a Bible discussion. You decide to use the "Go on a God Hunt" skill on a particular passage, and spend the whole 20 minutes doing the exercise and discussing it.

Another week, you might want to do a more practical approach. You pick up the "Implications and Benefits" skill and use it to launch a short discussion. Or you choose two of the skills to use together.

The rest of this guide will assume you're focusing on the first way to approach the study: by using it to teach Bible study skills.

Study Format

Each week includes an introduction, followed by a practice segment in each Bible study phase:

- 1 skill for investigation
- 1 skill for interpretation
- 1 skill for engaging

I've assumed a group session of 90 minutes minimum:

- 15 minutes for settling in and introduction
- 60 minutes on the three study segments (20 minutes each)
- 15 minutes for closing discussion or prayer

This book is designed to be used as a workbook that leads group members through each week's study.

Introduction. For the introduction, a group member can read aloud the week's introduction that I've written, or you might simply draw attention to what especially stood out to you from it.

Study Segments. For each study segment, explain the skill — or simply read the instructions aloud — and then dive in and do the "Practice It" portion together.

I'd suggest working on the study segments as a group (or smaller groups) rather than having people work individually. As you move into weeks three or four, you might want to vary the format by doing some segments individually or without breaking into groups. In a group that has some potential leaders, you can also vary the format by passing leadership around the group.

Keep your eye on the clock during these study practice times, and move the group on to the next segment after 20 minutes. You may need to say, "We could keep going with this discussion for a long time, but even though there's more to say, let's go ahead and turn the page to the next phase of this study."

Wrap Up. Use the time at the end of the study to process personal applications, either by discussing as a group or by giving people time to listen to God quietly and individually.

Choosing Your Bible Passage

As the leader, you'll need to decide what passage to study with your group. To get started, first see the general thoughts under "Bible Passages to Use" at the front of the book (in the "How to Use This Study" pages).

In addition, when you're working with a group, it's especially important to keep the Bible portion you're covering short. If there's one mistake I've made in teaching people these skills, it's in underestimating how much time it takes a group of people to read through a passage and get a basic orientation to it. I've chosen passages that are too long, and then halfway through the meeting have had to alter on the fly and narrow down the segment we're studying.

It's better to give groups smaller portions and plenty of time to do them. You can always say, "Focus on verses 14-17, and then, if you have extra time, move on to verses 18-22."

Rule of thumb: The more people you're guiding, the shorter your passage should be.

Leading the Study Segments

During the study segments, you'll need to pace the group to make sure they keep moving and keep the discussion focused.

Dividing into smaller groups. A group of two to five members can do all the practices together.

If you have more members, I'd suggest you divide into smaller groups of two to four who do the study segments together. Sometimes, I've assigned people into groups so I can mix people new to the Bible into groups with those who have a little more experience. I want to make sure everyone gets to participate and feels helped and encouraged. I particularly don't want people new to the Bible or people who feel intimidated by "study" to be put on the spot or feel isolated.

On a practical note, if I have a large number of people, I divide people into groups first, get everyone's attention again, and then explain the study segment. If you explain everything before the movement and distraction of breaking into groups, people tend to forget what they are supposed to do, and you'll field a lot more questions. You can also just read the study segment instructions aloud together to ensure everyone is on the same page.

While the groups are working, you can join a group or move from group to group listening in and offering suggestions as needed.

Sharing results. After the groups have worked together and time is up, ask one person from each group to report their findings to the larger group. If you have quite a few smaller groups, instead of asking for a report from each one, you can ask generally, "What was a key thought you discovered?" Then, invite more groups to share by asking, "Who found something else?" and, "What else did you notice?"

Discuss the findings a little and then draw back from the passage to point out what they learned about studying the Bible. You can ask questions such as, "What did you learn about finding context?" or, "Why was it important to take the time to find out what the passage meant *then*?" Pulling back like this from the content of the passage itself keeps the discussion focused on learning *how* to study.

Note: Some of the "engage" segments will be more personal and will ask participants to be open and honest about their responses to the passage. You may want to give quiet, individual space to do these, and then open up for discussion without requiring people to share what happened between them and God.

You may get more open responses at these times if you share first and model that it's OK to be genuine. I've found people often feel a great relief when they know I have wrestled with a passage, been bored by it, or have been reluctant to apply it. It gives them freedom to know that I don't expect them to have a "nice Christian" response to everything in the Bible; it's OK to wrestle with God about what is there.

Guiding the Discussion

Keep the following thoughts in mind as you guide the group's discussions.

Know where to focus. I mentioned that you can use this study to learn a set of skills or you can use it as a framework to provide Bible content for your group. Even if you're using the first approach, your group members will (naturally) lose focus on the tools or skills and start to focus on the passage itself. They will get involved in discussing this or that point in a passage and forget that they are learning the basics of *how* to study.

To ensure group members learn the Bible study *process*, you'll need to pull them out of the intense focus on the particulars of a passage and point out the study skill you're practicing. You can say, "Remember that we don't have time in this group meeting to sort out all these questions. We're just using this passage as a practice for learning how to study. Right now, we're learning to find the context of a passage. What else did you notice about the context?"

Keep the study phases separate, and emphasize investigation. Perhaps the biggest skill to learn in Bible study is to spend enough time with the passage itself, observing what is there. Few of us have learned how to do this. The investigation phase is central. Allow plenty of focus for it, and remind group members of the need for it.

Expect that people in your group will jump directly to interpretations or applications without realizing what they are doing. This is very natural, because most of us do more personal Bible reading than study. There, we tend to focus on personal application. Help group members make the distinction between investigating a passage and interpreting it.

At times, you will need to take charge of the discussion and pull the focus back to the Bible study phase you are in: "That's an interesting thought, and we may want to spend more time there later when we talk about how to interpret this passage or engage with God about it. But for now, we're doing investigation. Remember that we want to stick with simply looking to see what is actually there. Later, we'll talk about what it means for us personally."

Help group members be learners — not teachers. You may have some people who have a great deal of Bible knowledge. They may bring up lots of background information or begin "teaching" the group out of what they already understand about the passage (or about other passages that this one brings to mind).

At your first meeting, before any discussion, tell your group: "Sometimes we'll hit an area where you may have a lot of Bible knowledge. It's going to be really tempting for us just to 'teach' each other out of what we already know. Please don't! Remember that our goal is to learn how to study, not to share what we already know. When we come to a point where you have a lot of information, you'll want to share your knowledge with us. At that point, please keep yourself from speaking up. Instead, join in with helping other group members learn how to discover for themselves." A statement such as this helps set expectations.

As you get into the weeks of the study, if someone brings up a lot of information they've already learned, thank them for the background, and then transition back into helping *everyone* learn how to study. You can do this by telling the group how they, too, could find the type of information the person just shared: "When we're doing Bible study, you can find that type of information by looking up the cross references in your Bible, or by checking out the entry in a Bible dictionary." Then get back to the passage: "What else can we see from the passage itself, if we don't have access to that resource?"

If you don't know what Bible study resource might be useful, just tell the group, "I'm not sure I'd know how to find that information. What type of resource do you think we could use here?" Remember: You're all learners together; you don't have to have all the answers.

Dealing with unresolved questions. This study may raise questions regarding your passage that simply cannot be resolved in the short group time you have.

At the first group meeting, prepare your group for this: "We're going to raise more questions than we will be able to answer. That's OK. It's going to be uncomfortable, but there will be times we will cut a discussion short and move on, leaving questions hanging out there, unanswered. Our goal isn't to come to a complete knowledge of this passage, but to learn how to get started studying the Bible."

In later weeks, when you get stuck during a discussion, you can remind them, "Remember that we're learning how to study, and we won't always have time to follow through on these questions." Or you can tell them what kind of resource might help them: "You can look up *propitiation* in a Bible dictionary; it will describe some more information for you."

And sometimes, we simply have to live with unresolved issues: "Christians disagree about this passage, and we won't be able to come to a clear conclusion about it in the space we have."

If you don't feel confident in your ability to handle more difficult questions, identify a mentor in your church before you begin. Who will be able to help you if you get stuck? (Don't overlook some of the quieter or older men and women in the background who have been walking with God for a long time; they can be great sources of wisdom and knowledge about the Bible, and would be honored to share with someone who wants to learn.)

Bibles to Use

For Bible-study beginners, I emphasize studying with a paper book (not an app), because doing so means they are inherently studying in context. They see other Bible books as they flip through to find their passage, and they can't escape seeing the paragraphs before and after the portion they are studying.

I will bring extra Bibles to group meetings if I think some group members may only use a Bible app or may only have a paraphrased Bible version. If you don't have extra Bibles, you may be able to borrow some from your church office or from friends.

Though I want people to have a Bible in front of them and get used to using it, I also like to give them a photocopy or printout of the passage we'll be studying. That way they can freely mark all over it without being concerned about whether they want those marks permanently in their Bibles.

It's fine if group members have different Bible versions from each other — in fact, they'll learn by comparing versions.

Study Resources

I try to keep the study resources we use during the group meeting to a minimum. Especially if you have a larger group, you could spend a lot of time simply explaining and demonstrating how to use a book, an app, or a website, and lose track of studying the passage itself.

If there is a resource I think is absolutely necessary to what we're doing, I try to give everyone a photocopy or printout of the one page we need — sometimes I'll even circle the part of the page I want them to focus on. Most Bible study resources are dense with information, and I want to make it as simple as possible for people to know what to look at and where to focus (without eating up a lot of group time doing so).

Homework

You can do this study entirely in your group time, without homework. However, if you would like to encourage people to dig in on their own between group meetings, ask them to choose a passage of their own to study — or give them a passage.

Then, after each week's session, they can go back to the three study segments they practiced with the group and use them on their passage at home. This will reinforce what they've done in a group, and give them time to use some background resources.

ACKNOWLEDGMENTS

Many thanks to . . .

The wonderful people at Our Lord's Community Church who encouraged and supported me as I taught and wrote this material. Particularly my community group, who said, "Teach us — please!" And to my classes who patiently and enthusiastically worked their way through the rough material with me.

Darcy, Esther, and Kris, who all said, "Yes, write it, already!" You gave me confidence and coffee — necessary fuel. And to John, with whom I first taught this course.

The pilot groups in Panama and elsewhere who looked past all the typos and gave me their helpful responses. And to Cynthia, for your insightful feedback and friendly encouragement.

To Diane and Mary Jane, for your eagle eyes on the manuscript. (I promise, any remaining errors are firmly my fault.)

My family for your support, and to Dad, for demonstrating a keen, life-long love of God's Word.

And to my Father and Friend. Thanks for all the talks, the generosity, the encouragement, and the urging on. Only You know how many of the ideas (the really good ones) in this study are Yours. Thanks for letting Me talk with You and others about Your Book.

ABOUT THE AUTHOR

CONNIE WILLEMS is an author, editor, and personal coach. She grew up in a home infused with the Bible — and in a Bible church. Over the years, God worked her head knowledge about His book down into heart knowledge about Him.

She honed her Bible study skills through personal study and through writing studies as an editor of *Discipleship Journal,* a senior editor at NavPress, and an author for Community Bible Study.

Connie is the author with Buddy Westbrook of *Come Talk with Me: Developing the Skill of Communicating with God.*

Connie loves a great conversation over a great meal with great friends, time in her beloved mountains, and hanging out with God, wherever He is. She currently lives in Oklahoma City, Oklahoma.

MORE RESOURCES

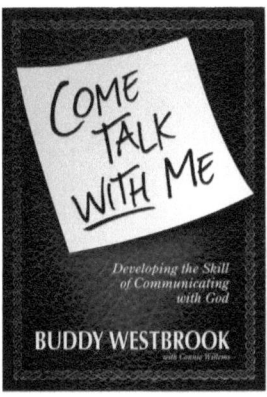

Come Talk with Me
Developing the Skill of Communicating with God
Buddy Westbrook with Connie Willems

This is not a book you simply read; this is a book you do. *Come Talk with Me* will walk you step-by-step into relational conversation with God. Through instruction, stories, examples, practical exercises, and hands-on coaching, you will learn how to hear God accurately and relate with Him deeply. You will discover how to wrestle with Him, enjoy Him, and receive His incredible parenting, friendship, understanding, care, and direction. If you want to engage with God more personally and closely, *Come Talk with Me* will show you how.

Resources, Training, and Coaching
Connie delights in helping busy, committed Christians discover sustainable, intentional life, work, and ministry with God as their Father and Friend.

To find more information, visit
RealLifeDiscovery.com

www.ingramcontent.com/pod-product-compliance
Lightning Source LLC
Chambersburg PA
CBHW020621300426
44113CB00007B/737